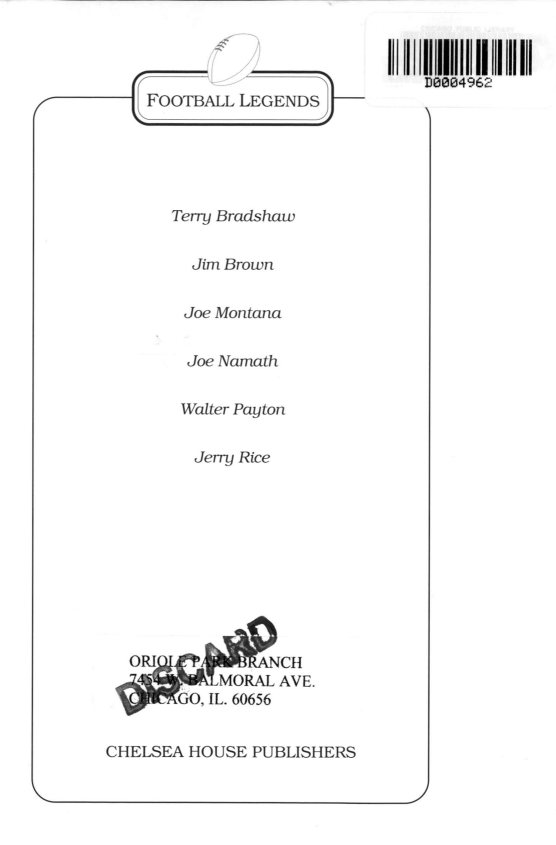

FOOTBALL LEGENDS

Terry Bradshaw

Jim Brown

Joe Montana

Joe Namath

Walter Payton

Jerry Rice

CHELSEA HOUSE PUBLISHERS

JOE MONTANA

Paul Wiener

Introduction by
Chuck Noll

CHELSEA HOUSE PUBLISHERS
New York · Philadelphia

Produced by Daniel Bial and Associates
New York, New York.

Picture research by Alan Gottlieb
Cover illustration by Jon Weiman

1 3 5 7 9 8 6 4 2

Wiener, Paul
    Joe Montana / Paul Wiener.
    p. cm. — (Football legends)
    Includes bibliographical references (p.   ) and index.
    ISBN 0-7910-2453-9
    1. Montana, Joe, 1956–   —Juvenile literature. 2. Football players—
United States—Biography—Juvenile literature.
    [1. Montana, Joe, 1956–   .   2. Football players.]
    I. Title. II. Series.
    GV939.M59W54 1994
    796.332'092—dc20
    [B]   94-1350
                                                                 CIP
                                                                 AC

CONTENTS

A WINNING ATTITUDE

Chuck Noll

Don't ever fall into the trap of believing, "I could never do that. And I won't even try—I don't want to embarrass myself." After all, most top athletes had no idea what they could accomplish when they were young. A secret to the success of every star quarterback and sure-handed receiver is that they tried. If they had not tried, if they had not persevered, they would never have discovered how far they could go and how much they could achieve.

You can learn about trying hard and overcoming challenges by being a sports fan. Or you can take part in organized sports at any level, in any capacity. The student messenger at my high school is now president of a university. A reserve ballplayer who got very little playing time in high school now owns a very successful business. Both of them benefited by the lesson of perseverance that sports offers. The main point is that you don't have to be a Hall of Fame athlete to reap the benefits of participating in sports.

In math class, I learned that the whole is equal to the sum of its parts. But that is not always the case when you are dealing with people. Sports has taught me that the whole is either greater than or less than the sum of its parts, depending on how well the parts work together. And how the parts work together depends on how they really understand the concept of teamwork.

Most people believe that teamwork is a fifty-fifty proposition. But true teamwork is seldom, if ever, fifty-fifty. Teamwork is *whatever it takes to get the job done.* There is no time for the measurement of contributions, no time for anything but concentrating on your job.

One year, my Pittsburgh Steelers were playing the Houston Oilers in the Astrodome late in the season, with the division championship on the line. Our offensive line was hard hit by the flu, our starting quarterback was out with an injury, and we were having difficulty making a first down. There was tremendous pressure on our defense to perform well—and they rose to the occasion. If the players on the defensive unit had been measuring their contribution against the offense's contribution, they would have given up and gone home. Instead, with a "whatever it takes" attitude, they increased their level of concentration and performance, forced turnovers, and got the ball into field goal range for our offense. Thanks to our defense's winning attitude, we came away with a victory.

Believing in doing whatever it takes to get the job done is what separates a successful person from someone who is not as successful. Nobody can give you this winning outlook; you have to develop it. And I know from experience that it can be learned and developed on the playing field.

My favorite people on the football field have always been offensive linemen and defensive backs. I say this because it takes special people to perform well in jobs in which there is little public recognition when they are doing things right but are thrust into the spotlight as soon as they make a mistake. That is exactly what happens to a lineman whose man sacks the quarterback or a defensive back who lets his receiver catch a touchdown pass. They know the importance of being part of a group that believes in teamwork and does not point fingers at one another.

Sports can be a learning situation as much as it can be fun. And that's why I say, "Get involved. Participate."

CHUCK NOLL, the Pittsburgh Steelers head coach from 1969–1991, led his team to four Super Bowl victories—the most by any coach. Widely respected as an innovator on both offense and defense, Noll was inducted into the Pro Football Hall of Fame in 1993.

1

THE MIRACLE WORKER

Only 190 seconds remained in Super Bowl XXIII. The San Francisco 49ers trailed the Cincinnati Bengals 16-13. The 49ers had possession of the football on their own 8 yardline. In order to score a touchdown and win, the 49ers would have to move the ball virtually the entire length of the field in a relatively short period of time. This would be their last chance.

The sellout crowd of 85,129 that packed Miami's Joe Robbie Stadium to watch the game on that January 22, 1989, wondered if San Francisco's legendary quarterback, Joe Montana, could lead his team to yet another dramatic come-from-behind victory. Tens of millions of television viewers from around the world had similar thoughts. After all, Joe Montana was "The Comeback Kid."

Montana's nickname was well deserved. In college, he had led Notre Dame University to several breathtaking last-second victories. Perhaps

Joe Montana is surrounded by the media prior to Super Bowl XXIII in 1989.

9

none was more memorable than the 1979 Cotton Bowl. In that game, Montana, ill with a fever, came onto the field with 7:37 left to play and his team trailing the University of Houston by 22 points. He proceeded to lead the Fighting Irish to an extraordinary 35-34 victory.

Montana's clutch performances continued after he became a professional football player. His greatest moment may have come in the 1982 National Football Conference title game against the Dallas Cowboys when he threw a brilliant pass to Dwight Clark with only seconds left to win the game. Montana's connection with Clark became known to football fans as "The Catch."

Cincinnati Bengals head coach Sam Wyche knew not to feel too confident as Montana took control of the ball on the 49ers' 8 yardline with time running out in Super Bowl XXIII. As the 49ers' quarterback coach in the early 1980s, Wyche had witnessed the Comeback Kid win numerous games with last minute heroics. In fact, only the season before, Wyche watched as Montana defeated his Bengals on a last second touchdown pass to Jerry Rice.

Montana, who was calling his own plays, decided to take advantage of the Bengals' man-to-man coverage with a hurry-up offense. He began the final drive by passing over the middle to running back Roger Craig for 8 yards and then to tight end John Frank for 7 more yards and a first down. Two runs by Craig brought the ball to San Francisco's 35 yardline with 1:54 to play. The 49ers had covered slightly less than one third of the distance they needed to go and had taken up slightly over one third of the time that had been left on the clock.

Montana connected with Rice, his favorite receiver, on the left sideline for 17 yards, and then to Craig over the middle for 13 more yards and another first down. The ball was on Cincinnati's 35 yardline.

Suddenly, the excitement began to overwhelm Montana. He had been yelling as loudly as he could to try to make himself heard over the deafening roar of the crowd and he momentarily had trouble catching his breath. Wisely, Montana tossed an intentionally incomplete pass. This stopped the clock and allowed him to regain his composure.

Montana's next pass went over the middle to Craig. However, a penalty called on 49ers' center Randy Cross nullified the play. The ball was brought back to the Cincinnati 45 yardline.

Montana kept his cool. He fired a pass over the middle to Rice, who was surrounded by two Bengal defenders, cornerback Lewis Billups and safety Ray Horton. The ball was thrown perfectly, and the speedy Rice evaded Billups and Horton and surged to the Bengals' 18 yardline for a first down.

Montana dropped back again to throw and found Craig running a cross pattern from right to left. Craig was tackled at the 10 yardline with only 39 seconds left in the game. The 49ers called a time-out.

During the time-out, 49ers' broadcaster Joe Starkey remarked, "It's such a sight to watch this, whether it happens or not. To watch Joe Montana do this for so many years. To watch this absolute surgeon on the football field, one of the all-time greats do his thing again. It's almost like poetry."

Coach Bill Walsh called a play designed for Craig. But Craig, who was supposed to line up on the left side, lined up on the right side by mistake. After the ball was snapped, Montana first checked Craig, and then Rice. Both were tightly covered. Montana, with his extraordinary ability to improvise with the football, then noticed wide receiver John Taylor momentarily free in the end zone. He rifled a pass to Taylor for the winning touchdown.

"The Drive," as the final 190 seconds of this historic Super Bowl game became known, was in many ways typical of Montana's style of play. He did not try to win the game with one long, desperate pass. Rather, he opted for gains of 8, 10, and 12 yards, because such short passes were much more likely to succeed.

Montana's winning strategy demonstrated his ability to keep his opponents off-balance. During the Drive, he passed to not one but four of his teammates: Rice, Craig, Frank, and Taylor. Several of these passes were thrown towards the sidelines. But many were tossed up the middle, a gutsy tactic for a quarterback whose team is trailing near the end of a game because the game clock does not stop until the ball-carrier runs out of bounds.

Finally, Joe's remarkable composure had inspired his teammates with confidence. As Wyche noted after the game, "I don't know of anybody who can play as well in the clutch as Montana." Or, as center Randy Cross declared, "As far as Joe Montana's concerned, I hope people will finally stop saying they rate him with the best. He *is* the best. There's never been a better big-game quarterback."

Montana's performance in Super Bowl XXIII was especially dramatic because he had experienced such a difficult regular season.

Capping "The Drive," John Taylor leaps high off the ground as cornerback Rickey Dixon despairs.

Plagued by various injuries, he had been benched on and off, much to his dismay. With the 49ers struggling to make the playoffs, Coach Walsh finally handed Montana back the starting quarterback job. Montana responded by leading his team into the playoffs with four straight regular season wins and ultimately to its great victory in the Super Bowl. He was indeed the Comeback Kid.

2

MONONGAHELA JOE

Joe Montana was born on June 11, 1956, in New Eagle, Pennsylvania, and raised in the small western Pennsylvania town of Monongahela, 30 miles upriver from Pittsburgh. Monongahela is a working-class community of approximately 6,000 inhabitants, surrounded by steel mills, coal mines, and farms.

It is also located in the heart of football country. Residents of this part of Pennsylvania rabidly support the Pittsburgh Steelers and the college football teams of Penn State University and the University of Pittsburgh. High school football games are also very well attended.

Perhaps it is not surprising then that western Pennsylvania has produced so many of the game's greatest quarterbacks, including Dan Marino, the Miami Dolphins' all-pro; Johnny Unitas, the Baltimore Colts' Hall of Famer; Joe Namath, the New York Jets' Super Bowl hero;

Joe Montana drives to the hoop as a high school star point guard.

and Terry Hanratty, who played for Notre Dame and was Joe Montana's boyhood hero.

Joe was an only child. Although his parents had little extra money to spare, they provided a loving, warm home for their son. When Joe was three, his father, Joseph Montana, Sr., quit his job as a telephone equipment installer and became the manager of a finance company in Monongahela in order to spend more time with his family. Joe's mother, Theresa, worked as a secretary at the same company.

Joseph Senior, who had played football, basketball, and baseball in the Navy, instilled a passion for sports in his son at an early age. Each day, after elementary school, Joe would sit on the front steps of his family's two-story frame house waiting for his father to return from work. The two would spend hours together working on young Joe's skills as a quarterback. First, dad would swing a tire back and forth and Joe would try to fire a football through the center of the tire. Then they would work on pass patterns and on setting Joe up to throw properly. Among other things, Joe learned from his father how to move straight back rather than to the side as soon as he caught the center's snap in order to evade the opposing team's defensive tacklers.

Joe first participated in organized sports at age eight for a peewee football team called the Monongahela Little Wildcats. He played quarterback and even at this age was an extraordinarily accurate passer.

Joe played organized sports all year round—football in the fall, basketball in the winter, and baseball in the spring and summer. Of these sports, basketball was his favorite since it demanded total involvement by every player on the court. In addition, he loved the dodging and faking involved in playing basketball.

Joe's father organized the basketball games. He rented a gym several nights a week and created a league with 10 teams. Joseph Senior and some of his friends taught basketball fundamentals to the participating youngsters, who chipped in $2 each to cover costs. During Joe's junior high school years, his father organized an all-star basketball team that participated in regional tournaments. Joe played the guard position.

At age 10, Joe began to experience sports burnout. One day, several weeks after football practice had started, he told his father that he wanted to quit playing football and join the Cub Scouts instead. His father replied, "If you want to quit, you can. But only after you've finished playing out the year. I don't want you ever to quit anything you've already started." Joe decided not to quit.

By the time Joe joined the football team at Ringgold High School during his sophomore year he was tall and thin—six feet tall, but weighing only 165 pounds. Despite Joe's multi-sport reputation—he had starred in football, baseball, basketball, and track and field in junior high— the football coach kept Joe on the bench for most of his sophomore year. Coach Abramski felt that Joe was too young and skinny, and he mocked Joe by calling him "Joe Banana." In practice, Abramski encouraged other players to hit Joe hard in order to toughen him. The coach's decision not to play Joe infuriated Joe's father, who had many unsuccessful arguments about this with Abramski.

During the summer, Joe played basketball and other sports to stay in shape, although he

Montana, second from the left in the rear, was also a stand-out baseball player in high school.

refused to take part in a weightlifting program that Coach Abramski had suggested. Joe's father would not allow his son to get a job during high school, preferring that he concentrate on sports.

After the Ringgold Rams were routed in the opening game of the 1972 season, Coach Abramski finally decided to change quarterbacks. Given a chance to start in a big game against powerhouse Monessen High School, Joe excelled. The junior completed 12 of 22 passes for 223 yards and 4 touchdowns. The Rams went on to post a 4-3-2 record. In Joe's senior year, the Rams finished 8-2, and Joe was named a high school all-American quarterback.

Despite all of the frustration and abuse that he had suffered, Joe felt that he had learned a lot playing for Coach Abramski. In particular, he credits his high school coach for teaching him how to throw on the run and how to "feel the color," that is, scramble free from defenders.

Joe also played center, forward, and guard for Ringgold High School's basketball team. Sometimes, he played all three positions in the same game. He had so much natural jumping ability that he could stand directly underneath the basket, leap up, and dunk the ball two-handed. During his junior year, he averaged 11 points a game, and his team competed for the state championship.

On the baseball diamond, Joe played all nine positions. His batting average was just under .500.

During Joe's junior and senior years of high school, he received recruiting letters from almost every major college football program in the country. Scouts crowded the Ringgold High School stadium to watch him play. Joe visited several schools, including the University of Georgia, Boston College, the University of Minnesota, Penn State, Pittsburgh, and Notre Dame.

He also was offered a basketball scholarship from North Carolina State University. Joe felt honored, but he realized that since he stood only 6'2", his chances of playing professional basketball were slim. Joe also was invited to a major league baseball camp. He did so well that he was asked to participate in a second camp, which he did not attend. His best position was shortstop.

Joe had long nursed two sports-related dreams. The first was to play for Notre Dame. The second was to become a professional athlete—preferably as a quarterback. When Notre Dame offered Joe a football scholarship, the first of his dreams was about to come true.

3

AN IRISH HERO

Joe had a hard time making the transition from Monongahela to South Bend, Indiana. He was homesick during his freshman year of college. He also had to adjust to the reality that he was just another quarterback battling for scarce playing time. Indeed, during Joe's freshman year, the Notre Dame football team, which had won the national championship the year before, had no fewer than 11 quarterbacks, including seven freshmen! Moreover, Joe began his college career ranked only eighth on this depth chart. In other words, the coaches considered seven other Notre Dame quarterback better than Joe Montana.

Notre Dame's freshmen football players are automatically placed on the junior varsity team. Yet even on this team, Joe rarely received playing time during his initial season. The coaches

Hard to believe, but when Joe Montana first arrived at Notre Dame University, seven other quarterbacks were presumed to be better than he. Here Number 3 matches form with some of his rivals.

recognized that he was a talented passer but felt he did not work hard enough in practice or take football seriously. Joe also soon discovered that big-time college football players consistently tackle hard, even in practice. The grueling daily practices toughened him up, and Joe learned how to take punishment and keep on going.

Despite all his difficulties on the football field, Joe never stopped believing that he was Notre Dame's best quarterback. As he wrote in his autobiography, *Audibles*, "Once you start thinking that people are better than you, you start giving up. That's when you are destined to stay on the bottom."

The middle of Joe's freshman year was marked by his marriage to Kim Moses, his high school sweetheart. After the wedding, Joe moved into an off-campus apartment with Kim, who found a job as a secretary in the Notre Dame sports information office.

Joe began the 1975 season as Notre Dame's number-two-ranked quarterback. He had rocketed up the depth chart by impressing Notre Dame's new head football coach, Dan Devine—who succeeded the legendary Ara Parseghian—with consistently outstanding practice performances during the previous spring.

During the third game of the season, against Northwestern University, Rick Slager, Notre Dame's starting quarterback, suffered an injury. With his team trailing 7-0, Devine brought Joe into a varsity game for the first time. The sophomore played extremely well and led the Fighting Irish to a 31-7 victory. He threw his first college touchdown pass, a 14-yarder down the middle, and scored the final touchdown of the game when he faked a pitch and ran in from the 6 yardline.

Joe remained the backup quarterback for the rest of the 1975 season. He did, however, lead Notre Dame to two thrilling come-from-behind victories that season.

The first was at the University of North Carolina. With just over five minutes left in the game and Notre Dame trailing 14-6, Joe was sent onto the field. In just five plays, he completed a 73-yard drive that resulted in a touchdown. He then passed for the 2-point conversion to tie the score. The winning play came with just over a minute left in the game. With the ball stuck on the Notre Dame 20, Joe looked over the defense and barked out a play different from the one sent in by the coach. He then delivered a perfect pass to his receiver, Ted Burgmeier, who ran for the winning score.

Joe followed up this performance with an even more dramatic effort the next week against the Air Force Academy. Air Force led 30-10 in the second half when Devine sent Joe into the game. In only eight minutes, Joe threw two touchdown passes, and Notre Dame walked off with a 31-30 victory. The Fighting Irish finished the year with an 8-3 record. Joe was becoming known as the Comeback Kid.

Off the field, Joe was struggling academically. At Ringgold High, he had been a "B" student. But Notre Dame demanded significantly greater efforts, and Joe found it difficult to balance football, marriage, and schoolwork. In his sophomore year, Joe was placed on academic probation. He would have to improve his grades soon, or he would be ineligible to play college football.

In a practice before the 1976 season, Joe separated his shoulder. Notre Dame "red shirted" him for the year, which meant he could not play during the season but he could keep his eligibility to play two more years of varsity football. One important benefit of not playing was that Joe was able to spend more time on his classwork. His grades improved markedly, and he was removed from academic probation.

Joe was extremely upset when he began the 1977 season as Notre Dame's third-string quarterback. He felt that he had already proved himself and now that he was healthy, he wanted to return as a starter.

In the third game of the season, against Purdue University, Joe finally saw some action. Notre Dame was trailing 24-12 and there was less than two minutes remaining in the third quarter. The Notre Dame fans, who had not forgotten the Comeback Kid, cheered wildly. Joe did not disappoint them. After a Notre Dame field goal, he connected on a 13-yard pass to tight end Ken Macafee to tie the score. Then, with time running out, Joe tossed two long passes to set up the winning touchdown. In the 31-24 victory, the third-string quarterback completed 9 of 14 passes for a total of 154 yards.

After the Purdue win, Devine had no choice but to start Joe. With Montana at the helm, Notre Dame did not lose another game that season. This included a 49-17 whipping of a traditional rival, the University of Southern California (USC).

Montana impressed Devine with his attitude as well as his performance on the field. One day, late in the season, a newspaper attributed to Joe some critical remarks about Devine. That night, Joe knocked on Devine's door and apologized, explaining that he had not intended to criticize his coach.

With a 10-1 record and a number two rank-ing in the country, Notre Dame was invited to the Cotton Bowl in Dallas, Texas. Its opponent was the top-ranked and undefeated University of Texas. The Longhorns, boasting Earl Campbell, the running back who had won the Heisman Trophy that year (awarded to the best college player in the country) were the clear fa-vorites. Notre Dame's star player was Montana, who had thrown 11 touchdown passes in only nine games. Despite the odds and a hostile Texas crowd, the Irish won easily, 38-10. By winning, Notre Dame end-ed the season as the na-tional collegiate football champions.

Joe began the 1978 col-lege football season with high expectations, hop-ing for another national championship and pos-sibly a Heisman Trophy for himself. But Notre Dame lost its first two games and Joe threw two interceptions in each.

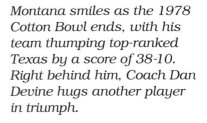

Montana smiles as the 1978 Cotton Bowl ends, with his team thumping top-ranked Texas by a score of 38-10. Right behind him, Coach Dan Devine hugs another player in triumph.

After that, the Fighting Irish reverted to form, losing only one more game the rest of the sea-son. One of these victories, against the Univer-sity of Pittsburgh, was won in classic Comeback Kid style. Pittsburgh led 17-7 with only eight minutes left. Montana took control of the game by completing seven straight passes for two touchdowns. Notre Dame won going away, 26-17. Even in Notre Dame's loss against USC, Montana almost pulled off another miracle.

Montana runs out of the arms of Houston's Fred Snell during the final drive that led to Notre Dame's 35-34 victory in the 1979 Cotton Bowl.

Again he helped the Irish overcome a massive, late-game deficit, only this time USC prevailed on a last-second field goal.

Yet Montana's most memorable college performance was undoubtedly in his last game for Notre Dame, the 1979 Cotton Bowl against the University of Houston. The game was played in almost unspeakable conditions. At game time, the temperature was 17 degrees, and 30-mile-an-hour winds made it feel like 10 degrees below zero. Only 10,000 fans stayed to watch the entire game; 40,000 ticketholders stayed home.

The field was covered with ice, and players had difficulty holding onto the ball. At halftime, Notre Dame was trailing badly. Joe's body temperature dropped to 96 degrees—well below the normal 98.6 degrees. He shook uncontrollably. When the second half resumed, Joe stayed in the lockerroom, drinking bouillon in a desperate attempt to recover.

By the fourth quarter, Houston led 34-12. Although his body was still partially numb, Joe decided that he had to continue playing. With a little under eight minutes left, he reentered the game.

Quickly, Joe completed seven of eight passes for two touchdowns. Still, Notre Dame trailed 34-28. The Fighting Irish got the ball back once more, to set the stage for the final play of the game: With only two seconds left, Montana, sensing an all-out rush, rolled right and connected on a touchdown pass to Kris Haines. Notre Dame won 35-34. It was one of the greatest comebacks in college football history.

Joe graduated in December 1979 with a degree in business administration and marketing. In the end, he was happy to be leaving Notre Dame. Joe had never really gotten along well with Devine, although he realized that he had learned a lot from his coach. Joe had also separated from his wife, as both realized they had gotten married too young.

Still, Joe had become a superstar at Notre Dame, probably the best quarterback the school had ever had. Now he was ready for the challenge of professional football.

4
LEARNING THE ROPES

Despite Montana's brilliant performance in his final two years at Notre Dame, many NFL scouts and coaches doubted that he would be successful as a professional quarterback. They felt that Joe—at 6'2" and 185 pounds—was too small for the NFL and that he did not have a strong enough arm. In addition, they worried about his reputation for not getting along with his coaches and for being injury-prone. Even those scouts who felt that Montana had enough talent eventually to play in the NFL admitted to doubts. No one projected that he would develop into the greatest quarterback of all time.

After graduation, Montana traveled around the country attending workouts with various teams prior to the NFL draft. One of the teams that Joe worked out with was the San Francisco 49ers. The 49ers had a newly signed head coach, Bill Walsh, and were looking to draft a quarterback because both its current quarter-

Welcome to the NFL! Big John Matuszak of the Oakland Raiders attempts to block Montana's pass.

backs, Steve DeBerg and Scott Bull, had recently undergone knee surgery. Joe immediately impressed both Walsh and Sam Wyche, San Francisco's quarterback coach.

As Walsh said later, "The first thing I noticed about Joe was his feet. He had very quick feet, and he could move real well." Walsh was also impressed by Joe's willingness to learn as well as his self-confidence and leadership qualities. He told Joe to keep in shape since Joe might be hearing from the 49ers on draft day.

And indeed, in the third round, with the 82nd pick overall, the San Francisco 49ers drafted Joe Montana. Three quarterbacks were picked in the first round ahead of him.

Montana was delighted to be chosen by the 49ers. Bill Walsh was known to prefer an offense based primarily on short and middle range passes, the type of passes that Joe threw best. Walsh, who had previously been the head football coach at Stanford University and before that an assistant coach with the San Diego Chargers and Cincinnati Bengals, had a reputation for developing young quarterbacks. Two of his prize pupils had been Dan Fouts and Ken Anderson, both of whom had become outstanding NFL quarterbacks. Joe also realized that as a young player he was more likely to receive playing time with a 49ers team which had finished the 1978 season with only a 2-14 record than he would with a more successful team.

Montana's first professional training camp was difficult. He had to learn over 100 of Bill Walsh's complicated plays, plus learn the moves

Early in his career, Montana had to earn his keep by holding the ball for field-goal attempts. Here, Joe watches as Ray Wersching splits the uprights.

of all the receivers. A major solace was Dwight Clark, also a rookie, and a 10th-round pick from Clemson University. They roomed together and quickly became good friends, and in years to come they would turn into a formidable quarterback-receiver duo.

Steve DeBerg started for San Francisco during Montana's rookie year. He had won the top spot by beating out veteran quarterback Jim Plunkett. Montana and DeBerg were road roommates during the 1979 season and a friendly but fierce competition developed between them.

Although the 49ers were a poor team in 1979, finishing once again with a 2-14 record, Montana received little playing time. Bill Walsh did not want Joe to lose his confidence playing for a bad team or to injure himself behind a weak 49ers' offense. For the season, Joe threw a total of only 23 passes. He completed 13 for 1 touchdown. In his only start, against the St. Louis Cardinals, he completed a mere 5 of 12 passes for 36 yards. Joe's major contribution that year was holding the football for Ray Wersching, San Francisco's kicker, on attempted field goals and extra points.

Off the field, Joe got married for a second time, to Cass Castillo, a stewardess. Joe and Cass bought a small ranch near San Francisco. To go with the ranch, they also purchased two Arabian horses.

Steve DeBerg began the 1980 season as the 49ers' starting quarterback. In the sixth game, however, DeBerg threw seven interceptions and the 49ers lost to the Dallas Cowboys 59-14. Walsh decided to make a change.

Joe shared the quarterback duties with DeBerg for the remainder of the season. His most impressive effort came in a game against the New Orleans Saints. At halftime, the Saints had a massive 28-point lead. But in the second half, led by Montana, San Francisco scored four touchdowns and then a winning field goal in overtime.

Joe threw for an extraordinary 258 yards in the second half, after accumulating only 27 in the first half. The comeback is still considered one of the greatest in NFL history.

The 49ers finished the 1980 season with a 6-10 record, a solid improvement over the previous two years. Although he did not play much in the early part of the season, Joe still managed to throw 15 touchdown passes. He also led NFL quarterbacks with a passing completion rate of 64.5 percent. To the surprise of many, Joe Montana was quickly developing into an outstanding professional quarterback.

Before the 1981 season, Walsh decided to make Joe Montana the 49ers' starting quarterback. To avoid any problems, San Francisco traded Steve DeBerg to the Denver Broncos. The trade boosted Montana's confidence since he now knew that Walsh believed in his ability to lead the team.

And Montana led the 49ers to a spectacular 1981 season. After dropping two of its first three games, San Francisco took the league by storm by winning 12 of its last 13 games. Two of these victories included a 45-14 rout of the mighty Dallas Cowboys and a 17-14 victory of the 1979 and 1980 Super Bowl champion Pittsburgh Steelers. Ironically, this was the first Steelers game that Joe, who had grown up an avid fan of the team, had ever attended.

Dwight Clark and Joe Montana became unlikely heroes for the San Francisco 49ers. Clark was drafted in the 10th round and Montana in the third round of the 1978 draft.

The 49ers' 13-3 record represented an amazing turnaround for a team that had compiled a 10-38 record over the past three seasons. A major factor in the team's success was its dominant offensive line of John Ayers, Randy Cross, Keith Fahnhurst, Fred Quillan, and Dan Audick. Another key factor to the team's fortunes was its improved defensive backfield, affectionately known as "Dwight Hicks and the Hot Licks." "The Hot Licks" consisted of Ronnie Lott, Carlton Williamson, and Eric Wright, all drafted by San Francisco in 1981. Lott eventually became the heart of the team's great defense and a perennial All-Pro choice.

Finally, before the 1981 season the Niners acquired two quality veteran players through trades: Fred Dean, a ferocious pass rusher, and Jack "Hacksaw" Reynolds, a linebacker.

The most important component to San Francisco's success was Joe Montana. He became a master of the play-action fake, one of Walsh's favorite devices, in which the quarterback faked a handoff to the running back before rolling out to throw a pass. He was creative enough to change a play at the line of scrimmage when needed. And, according to Walsh, he "may have [had] the greatest football instincts I have ever seen." Joe was brilliant at scrambling and throwing off-balance, so if Walsh's set play broke down, he could improvise and still lead his team downfield. In 1981, Joe again led the NFL in pass completion percentage at 63.9 percent. He also had the second-lowest interception rate in the league.

For the first time in eight years, the 49ers made the playoffs. San Francisco easily defeated the New York Giants, 38-24, and then faced Dallas. The Cowboys, known as "America's Team" because of their national popularity, had routed the Tampa Bay Buccaneers 38-0 in their playoff game and were expected to beat San Francisco, despite the Niners previous victory over them. Tension between the two teams rose when in a pre-game interview Ed "Too Tall" Jones suggested that the 49ers were more lucky than good.

The game was a nail-biting, seesaw battle. The lead changed back and forth several times before Dallas scored a touchdown to go ahead 27-21 with only 4:19 left in the game. The 49ers took over the ball on their own 11 yardline. In his autobiography *Audibles*, Joe described how he felt at that moment. "It was super gut-check time. I felt numb. I heard no noise. I didn't know where I was or who we were playing. All I saw was 89 yards between us and the end zone."

Dallas expected San Francisco to pass, and set in a formation of six defensive backs and only one linebacker. Walsh took advantage of this by calling a lot of running plays.

Behind Montana, the 49ers moved the ball to the Cowboys' 6 yardline. On second down, Joe had an excellent chance to throw a winning touchdown pass but he missed an open Freddie Solomon. There were only 58 seconds left in the game and Joe was desperately trying not "to choke," as he put it.

The third-down play was once again supposed to go to Solomon. Joe, however, quickly found himself pressured by three Cowboy defenders, including the enormous Too Tall Jones. Joe back-pedaled and raced to his right. At the last moment, he caught a glimpse of Dwight Clark cutting across the back of the end zone.

Joe faked a throw to get the charging lineman to stop running at him. He then threw the ball high and deep into the end zone, past a lot of traffic, and Clark made a spectacular outstretched, game-winning catch. This play, one of Joe Montana's greatest, became known simply as "The Catch." By the time Montana reached the locker room, he was so overcome by the excitement that he collapsed. He recovered several minutes later.

Super Bowl XVI featured the 49ers against the Cincinnati Bengals, who were led by Kenny Anderson. The 49ers dominated the first half and took a 20-0 lead into the lockerroom. Joe, who admitted that he was nervous before the game, completed 12 of 18 passes for 132 yards. One of their drives started at their 8 yardline and went for a touchdown. The 92-yard drive was the longest in Super Bowl history.

In the second half, the Bengals came charging back. But when they had a first down on San Francisco's 3 yardline and could not score on four straight plays, the Niners had the game wrapped up. Montana attempted only four passes in the second half but was still voted the Most Valuable Player. He thereby tied Joe Namath as the youngest quarterback ever to win a Super Bowl MVP Award. He also joined Namath as the only quarterback to win both a national championship in college and a Super Bowl. Joe Montana had become a superstar.

5
STRIKING BACK

Montana's performance in the playoffs transformed him into a media star. *Time* magazine, which rarely features sports figures, placed Joe on its cover. He appeared on interview programs for each of the three major television networks. He made several commercials. A San Francisco newspaper ran a contest in which Bay Area fans selected yet another nickname for Montana. (The winning entry was "Big Sky.") In addition, Joe signed a four-year contract with the 49ers worth approximately $1.5 million, a huge sum for a professional football player in the early 1980s.

The 49ers' 1982 season was a disaster. Petty jealousies emerged among the team's players and between the players and coaches. Many players seemed to lack the same drive to win that they had shown during the previous season. Rumors of drug use could be heard.

Joe Montana could run with the ball, as Perry Williams (right) of the New York Giants finds out—53 yards too late in the 1984 playoff game.

When the 49ers lost their first two regular season games, the internal bickering and finger pointing increased. The tension became even worse, however, when the football players' union, the National Football League Players' Association (NFLPA), called for a strike.

The strike, the first in NFL history, lasted for 57 days and resulted in the cancellation of seven 49ers' football games. Most of the team's players supported the strike. But Joe did not. He felt that the issues the union was striking for—a share of the owners' television revenue as well as a percentage of the club's profits from the sale of tickets, food, and souvenirs—were the wrong ones. Joe believed that the union should be fighting for a system of free agency, in which a player is free to sign with any team when his contract expires.

Although Joe insisted that he would favor a strike if the issue were free agency, many of his teammates were skeptical. They suspected that Joe did not want to strike because he would lose a lot of money under the huge contract that he had just signed. Indeed, Joe did lose approximately $140,000 in salary because of the strike. Even after it ended, bitterness remained. Some players refused to talk to their teammates because of the strike. The 49ers ended their season with a dismal 3-6 record.

Despite the disruptions of the strike and the 49ers' failure on the field, Joe finished the 1982 season with remarkably impressive numbers. He completed 61.5 percent of his passes for 17 touchdowns and only 11 interceptions. He set an NFL record by throwing for at least 300 yards in five consecutive games. And, against the St.

Louis Cardinals in his first game back after the strike, Joe threw for an eye-opening 408 yards.

It was also clear by this time that friction existed between Montana and Coach Walsh. Both men had huge egos and each had sought to take credit at the expense of the other for the team's success in 1981. Then, after the 49ers faltered in 1982, Walsh told the press that the team's players "didn't want to win as much as I did." In addition, Walsh hinted that Montana had become too distracted by his non-football activities, such as making commercials. These remarks angered Joe, who countered by maintaining that he always played his hardest and that he had never allowed personal matters to interfere with his performance as a football player.

San Francisco appeared to have bounced back when it opened the 1983 season by winning four of its first five games. Over this span, the Niners averaged more than 30 points a game and Joe felt that the team's offensive unit was playing even better than it had in 1981. After its strong start, however, the 49ers inexplicably began to struggle, especially at home in Candlestick Park. The team barely squeaked into the playoffs by winning its final three games. They finished the regular season with a 10-6 record.

San Francisco won a nailbiter over its first playoff opponent, the Detroit Lions. The game's deciding play was a field goal attempt Detroit missed with only 10 seconds left.

The Washington Redskins were up next, and they boasted three outstanding players in quarterback Joe Theismann, fullback John Riggins, and receiver Art Monk. The Redskins jumped out to a 21-0 first-half lead. In the second half, however, the 49ers stormed back to tie the score behind three Joe Montana touchdown passes, including a 76-yarder to Freddie Solomon. But the Redskins pulled out a 24-21 victory on a field goal kicked with only 40 seconds left.

The 49ers' loss to the Redskins was especially wrenching for Montana since Washington's winning field goal drive had been aided by several controversial penalty calls. Moreover, although Joe completed 27 of 48 passes for 347 yards in the game, his final pass attempt had been intercepted. Right after the loss, Montana vowed that the 49ers would win next year's Super Bowl.

Montana had a busy off-season. He signed a new contract with the 49ers that was worth over $6 million for six years. At the time, the contract made him the highest paid player in the NFL. He also divorced his second wife, Cass. A few months later, while shooting a razor commercial, he met Jennifer Wallace, an actress and model. Jennifer played the Schick Sheriff and Joe played a cowboy. They got married two years later.

San Francisco played up to its full potential in the 1984 season. They rolled over their opposition and ended with a 15-1 record, the first NFL team ever to win 15 games during the regular season. Many of these victories were by lopsided scores: 33-0 against the Los Angeles Rams, 41-7 against the Cleveland Browns, 35-3 against the New Orleans Saints, and 51-7 against the Minnesota Vikings. The 49ers also defeated the Redskins, avenging the previous year's heartbreaking playoff defeat.

A major reason for the team's excellent play was the development of two outstanding run-

ning backs, Wendell Tyler and Roger Craig. With a powerful new running game to complement his passing, Joe finished the season with a superb NFL quarterback rating of 102.9. The rating measures a quarterback's passing efficiency based on the percentage of touchdown passes per passing attempt, the percentage of completions per attempt, the percentage of interceptions per attempt, and the average yards gained per attempt. Joe also threw for a then career high of 28 touchdowns.

In the playoffs, the 49ers defeated the New York Giants 21-10 and then the tough Chicago Bears 23-0 to reach Super Bowl XIX. This set up

Roger Craig flies through the air after catching a first-down pass from Joe Montana. William Judson of the Miami Dolphins made the tackle during the 1985 Super Bowl.

a much-anticipated matchup between the 49ers and the Miami Dolphins, who were led by their quarterback Dan Marino.

The hype prior to the Super Bowl was enormous. The media focused heavily on Marino, who had led the Dolphins to a 16-2 record (including two playoff victories) in only his second year in professional football. At 23, he was the youngest quarterback ever to start an NFL playoff game.

Marino excelled at throwing the long downfield pass. During the regular season, he had tossed an amazing 48 touchdown passes, easily shattering the old NFL record of 36, and he had thrown seven more in Miami's two playoff wins. In addition, Marino had also accumulated over 5,000 passing yards during the regular season, an average of more than 300 passing yards per game.

Cornerback Ronnie Lott made sure Mark Clayton didn't hold on to this Dan Marino pass during Super Bowl XIX.

The intense media attention that Marino received before the Super Bowl angered Montana, who felt that his own personal accomplishments, as well as those of his teammates, were being slighted. As Joe remarked at the time, "You don't mind being overlooked that much, but sometimes the reporters forgot that there were two teams in the game. It got to all of us. Our accomplishments were being totally ignored, and for one of the few times in my career I was angry."

Despite expectations that the game would be close, San Francisco romped to victory by a score of 38-16. Marino attempted 50 passes and gained 318 yards in the air, but he was intercepted twice and sacked four times. Montana, playing one of his best games, was easily the superior quarterback on the day. Behind an offensive line that gave him great protection, he passed for three touchdowns. He also set several Super Bowl records, including most passing yards (331), most rushing yards by a quarterback (59), and most numbers of pass attempts without an interception (35).

Montana won his second Super Bowl MVP trophy, joining Hall of Famers Bart Starr and Terry Bradshaw as the only two-time MVP winners. He was also selected to play in the Pro Bowl, which is the NFL's post-season All-Star game.

In 1984, the Niners established themselves as the NFL's elite squad. And most observers now agreed that Montana was the game's best quarterback.

Joe experienced lower-back pain during training camp prior to the 1985 season. The doctors who examined him determined that he had been born with scoliosis, an irregular curvature of the spine. They also found that he had a twisted vertebra. Years of being hammered by 240-pound linebackers and 280-pound ends had clearly aggravated Joe's condition.

Montana exercised his back by walking in a swimming pool while wearing a special jacket to keep afloat. He missed a couple of exhibition games but returned for the 49ers' season opener, a 28-21 loss to the Vikings.

The Niners compiled a respectable 10-6 record in 1985, but five of their losses were by seven points or fewer. For the first time in his career, Joe was booed by the hometown fans, who had grown accustomed to seeing their team win practically every game. He also received several nasty letters from frustrated 49er fans. Montana reacted angrily, and sometimes publicly, to this criticism.

San Francisco edged into the playoffs by winning its last two regular season games against the Saints and Cowboys. Montana threw for over 300 yards in each of these must-win games.

Joe's 1985 statistics again were outstanding. He had two streaks of over 100 passes thrown without an interception. He led the NFC, and was ranked third in the entire NFL, in yards passing. He led the NFC in completions. He also finished the year with 27 touchdowns, second only to Dan Marino's 30.

During the week before the 49ers' playoff game against the New York Giants, Montana pulled an abdominal muscle. Over the next few days, he received eight injections. In pain for the entire game, Joe threw for 296 yards—but it was not enough. The Giants triumphed, 17-3. For the first time in over two years, an opponent had prevented the 49ers from scoring a touchdown. To make matters worse, Montana injured his shoulder in the game when Lawrence Taylor, the Giants' great linebacker, pounded him on a blindside hit. The injury kept Joe from playing in the Pro Bowl, though he had been named a starter.

Rookie Jerry Rice had made an immediate impact on the 49ers in 1985, accumulating nearly 1,000 pass-reception yards. In addition,

Roger Craig became the first player in NFL history to gain more than 1,000 yards rushing and 1,000 yards receiving in a single season.

But 1986 started with a crash for San Francisco. Early in the opening game against the Tampa Bay Buccaneers, Montana twisted his back severely as he scrambled on a pass play. He stayed in the game until a later play, when he was thrown to the ground. After being helped from the field, it was discovered he had ruptured a disk in his back. This is an extremely serious injury. A ruptured disk puts pressure on the nerves and causes a great deal of pain.

In a two-hour operation, the doctors removed part of the damaged disk from his back. They

Joe Montana had to be helped off the field after being knocked unconscious by Jim Burt in the 1987 playoff game against the New York Giants.

also widened his spinal cavity to correct a congenital problem. Although the operation was a success, in a post-surgery interview Dr. Arthur White said, "With proper rest and therapy, there's every chance that [Joe] could lead a normal life. I think there's very little chance he'll play football again." Many others agreed with the doctors, including some of his teammates.

Thousands of wellwishers called a Joe Montana hotline phone number and sent scores of letters and presents to his hospital. They knew Joe could retire a millionaire and expected that he'd never play again. They just wanted him to know that they supported him.

Only days after the operation, Montana started his rehabilitation program. At first, he could barely move, even with a walker. But soon he was was walking, then climbing stairs. Two weeks after the operation, he was running, swimming, and lifting weights. Three weeks later, he began training with the 49ers, initially in light drills only.

Fifty-five days after his back surgery, Joe Montana returned to the 49ers' starting lineup in a game against the Cardinals. He had missed eight games. Without him, the Niners had been mediocre, winning four, losing three, and tying one. As he took the field, Montana received a thunderous standing ovation from the fans at Candlestick Park. An electric chill went through the stadium.

In a storybook performance, Joe led his team to a 32-17 win. He completed 13 of 19 passes for 270 yards and threw three long touchdown passes—of 45, 40, and 44 yards—to Jerry Rice. Montana was on the field for nine possessions that day, and the 49ers scored on seven of them.

Despite being tackled hard several times, he did not get hurt.

The following week, against the Redskins, Montana again performed brilliantly. He tossed a career-high 60 passes for 441 yards. The game's best quarterback was back.

The 49ers went on to capture their fourth NFC West title since 1981. In the playoffs, they met the Giants for the second year in a row. During the second quarter, Montana was knocked unconscious by Jim Burt, the Giants' noseguard, and had to leave the game. Although Joe's back was not reinjured, he was chagrined to watch the Giants triumph easily by a score of 49-3. The Giants went on to win the Super Bowl.

Montana's fast return from a career-threatening injury was proof of his gritty competitiveness. After the season he was given the award for "courageous and inspirational play" by his teammates—and no one doubted that he had earned it.

6

TWO MORE RINGS

Two games into the 1987 season, the players' union called for another strike. This time the union sought free agency for NFL players when their contracts expired, the issue that Montana felt the union should have focused on during the 1982 strike.

After cancelling one game, the team owners brought in replacement players, who were not good enough to make NFL teams under normal circumstances, to play scheduled games. Joe honored the strike for the first replacement game but then crossed the picket line and played in the next two games, along with several other 49ers. The strike lasted 24 days.

Although it strained friendships on the 49ers, the strike did not perceptibly affect the team's performance on the football field. San Francisco finished the year at 13-2 (including a 3-0 record by its replacement team). Montana

Joe Montana and the 49ers romped in Super Bowl XXIV against the Denver Broncos. The game was a 55-10 laugher for San Francisco.

threw for 31 touchdown passes, which led the league and set a club record. And for the first time in his career he rated as the NFL's top passer with a rating of 102.1. At one point in the season he completed 22 consecutive passes, a league record.

In the first quarter of a game against the Chicago Bears, however, Montana strained his left thigh and had to leave the game. He was replaced by Steve Young, whom the 49ers had acquired a few months earlier from the Tampa Bay Buccaneers. Young, who had been a star quarterback at Brigham Young University (which was named after his great-great-grandfather), led the 49ers to an impressive 41-0 victory over the Bears. Because of his injury, Joe did not play in the team's remaining two games. Instead, with Young at quarterback, the 49ers thrashed their opponents by scores of 35-7 and 48-0.

Montana returned to the lineup in the opening playoff game. The Minnesota Vikings' pass rush was fierce and sacked Montana four times. He also threw a costly interception that resulted in a Viking touchdown. With a little more than six minutes remaining in the third quarter and the 49ers trailing 27-10, Walsh replaced Montana with Steve Young. It was the first time Joe had ever been benched, and he was furious. The Vikings went on to win 36-24 and San Francisco's season was over.

A quarterback controversy quickly grew during the offseason. Who would start in 1988: the 32-year-old Montana or the speedy 26-year-old Young? Killing rumors that Joe would be traded, the 49ers signed Montana to a five-year $10 million contract extension through 1992. But the money was not guaranteed. Joe would have to make the team each year.

Jerry Rice was Montana's favorite receiver. Here Mike Richardson of the Chicago Bears tries in vain to defend a pass in the 1989 NFC championship game. Rice not only came down with the ball, he ran 61 yards with it for a touchdown.

At first, Coach Walsh hedged on the question of who would be San Francisco's starting quarterback. Eventually, he told the media that Joe would start "as long as he's healthy." But this did not totally settle the controversy as Montana had suffered an assortment of injuries over the years and might never again be perfectly healthy. Most recently, after the 1987 season, he had undergone minor surgery on his sore right elbow.

Montana had a lot to celebrate after the 1990 Super Bowl. He was the first quarterback since Terry Bradshaw to lead his team to four championships, and the only man ever to win three Super Bowl MVP titles.

Walsh continued to waffle during the season, starting Montana one week and Young the next. For the first time in his career, Joe felt tentative on the field, knowing that one or two bad passes could lead to a seat on the bench, or a trade to another team.

Walsh maintained that he was using Joe cautiously in order to prevent him from aggravating various ailments to his back, knees, ribs, and elbow. Montana, however, felt Walsh was using this as an excuse to give Steve Young a fuller tryout. Young replaced Montana in eight games and started in three.

Finally, with the 49ers mired at 6-5 and unlikely to make the playoffs, Walsh handed Montana back the starting job. Joe responded by leading the 49ers to four wins in the last five games. For the sixth straight year, San Francisco made the playoffs. For the third straight year, the team captured the NFC West crown.

The 49ers routed the Vikings, the NFL's top defensive team 34-9, avenging the previous year's loss and breaking a string of three straight Niner first-round playoff losses. Joe threw three touchdown passes to Jerry Rice in the first half. He tossed three more touchdown passes in the 49ers' next playoff game, a 28-3 victory over the Bears in Chicago. Walsh called his team's performance "as great a game as we've had in many, many years."

Finally, San Francisco crowned its season by winning Super Bowl XXIII against the Cincinnati Bengals, as a result of the Drive. Montana set a Super Bowl record by passing for 357 yards in the game. It was the 19th time he had brought his team from behind in his pro football career.

The 49ers' Super Bowl victory made Walsh the second winningest coach in Super Bowl history (after Chuck Noll). Walsh decided to retire after the victory and joined NBC as a football commentator.

George Siefert, the team's defensive coordinator, was picked to replace Walsh. The 49ers adjusted quickly to the new coach. In 1989, they won their fourth straight NFC West Division title, with a 14-2 record. Montana had his greatest single season, and arguably the best season a quarterback has ever had in professional football. He compiled the highest single-season quarterback rating ever (112.4) and the third-highest pass completion percentage (70.2). The NFL named him its Most Valuable Player; *Sports Illustrated* named him "Player of the Year," and *The Sporting News* called him "Man of the Year."

The playoffs were no contest. The 49ers destroyed the Vikings 41-13 and the Rams 30-3. In the latter game, Montana completed 26 of 30 pass attempts.

Super Bowl XXIV against the Denver Broncos was an even bigger rout. In fact, the 55-10 final score was the most one-sided in Super Bowl history. Joe threw a Super Bowl record five touchdown passes and at one point he completed a Super Bowl record 13 consecutive passes. And for the third time in his career he was named Super Bowl MVP.

If there was any question before, the 1989 season seemed to have settled the matter. Joe Montana had established himself as one of the greatest quarterbacks of all time.

7

THE CHIEF

The 49ers' dominant play carried over into the 1990 season. The team won its first 10 games and finished with a league-leading 14-2 record. Montana had another excellent season. In one game he threw six touchdown passes and set a 49ers' record with 476 passing yards. *Sports Illustrated* named him "Sportsman of the Year," the first time a professional football player had won the award in 37 years. And for the second year in a row, Montana won the Associated Press NFL Most Valuable Player Award.

The Niners easily defeated the Redskins 28-10 in the first round of the playoffs. In the fourth quarter of the NFC championship game against the Giants, however, Joe broke a finger on his right hand when he was tackled by Leonard Marshall. The 49ers were leading 13-12 at the time. Steve Young had to finish the game, which the Giants won on a last-second field goal.

Montana leaving the field in 1993 after his last game as a San Francisco 49er.

Montana's finger healed quickly. However, he suffered a more serious injury just prior to the 1991 season. He was throwing a pass when he felt soreness in his right elbow. The soreness was diagnosed as a torn tendon, and in October Montana had surgery to reattach the tendon and muscles to a bone in the elbow. The surgery left him with a half-moon-shaped $2\frac{1}{2}''$ scar on the inside of his right elbow.

Montana's return to action in the 49ers' 1992 regular season finale against the Detroit Lions was a success. Although he only played in the second half of the game, he still completed 15 of 21 passes for 126 yards and two touchdowns. The best news was that his arm appeared strong and he showed few ill effects of a two-year layoff.

Joe's performance placed San Francisco in a bind. Steve Young had filled in for Joe spectacularly; in 1992 *he* was the league's MVP. Whenever a younger quarterback does well in place of an older one, football coaches usually start talking about "needing to go with youth" or "building for the future." But the 49ers clearly could win with either man, and Joe Montana wasn't just any older quarterback, he was perhaps the greatest quarterback of all time, a San Francisco legend. And he could still throw—and win.

After months of media speculation, in early April the 49ers announced that Young would start. The team gave Joe permission to work out a trade.

Montana was heavily courted by two teams, the Phoenix Cardinals and the Kansas City Chiefs. Although Phoenix offered him more money ($15 million for three years as opposed to

Kansas City's $10 million for three years), Joe opted for Kansas City. The Chiefs had reached the playoffs during each of the last three seasons and seemed on the verge of making the Super Bowl. Moreover, Kansas City's new offensive coordinator was Paul Hackett, who had been Montana's quarterback coach from 1983 to 1985. Hackett pledged that the Chiefs would run a 49ers' style offense in 1993.

At the last moment, the 49ers balked at trading Montana. The team even changed course and offered Joe the starting job. Joe declined. He knew that if he stayed in San Francisco the quarterback controversy would continue and that he might be benched at any time in favor of Young. Possibly the Niners were just trying to make Kansas City offer a better deal in the trade. Still, on April 20, 1993, the trade was effected.

Montanamania quickly swept Kansas City. Local stores sold four types of Montana T-shirts. One woman even asked Joe to sign the urn containing her husband's ashes before they were interred. The entire city seemed to expect Montana's greatness would rub off on them.

The 37-year-old Montana did not disappoint Kansas City's adoring fans. Although he missed several games due to a pulled left hamstring, the Chiefs finished the 1993 season with an impressive 11-5 record (8-3 when Joe started). In the games that Montana did play, he showed that even though his foot speed had slipped a little bit, he was still an outstanding quarterback who could move well in the pocket, throw with great accuracy, and play with intense competitiveness.

Once again, Montana's best performances came in the playoffs. In the Chiefs' opening

Montana, ignoring Buffalo Bills defensive end Bruce Smith, sets his eyes downfield as a quarterback for the Kansas City Chiefs.

game against the Pittsburgh Steelers, the Comeback Kid threw a game-tying touchdown pass on fourth down with less than two minutes remaining. Kansas City won 27-24 in overtime.

Montana struck again the following week against the favored Oilers in Houston. Trailing once again in the fourth quarter, the Chiefs scored 21 points over the final eight and a half minutes—including two Montana touchdown passes in a span of 54 seconds—to pull out a 28-20 victory.

The Buffalo Bills were next up against the Chiefs. The heavily-favored Bills had reached the Super Bowl in each of the three previous seasons (although they had lost each time). The media coverage in the week before the game was frenzied. Could Joe Montana lead his team to yet another improbable victory and a Super Bowl appearance?

No. Early in the third quarter, Montana received a blow to the head and sustained a concussion. He was helped off the field by team trainers and replaced by the quarterback he had replaced when he first joined the 49ers—Steve DeBerg. Buffalo won easily, 30-11.

Is Joe Montana really the greatest quarterback of all time? This is impossible to state for sure, partly because football styles have changed over the years. Johnny Unitas excelled during the "bump and grind" era, when the running game was more significant than it is today. Sid Luckman excelled back when football players were required to play both offense and defense.

Nevertheless, the records Montana has set prove that he has an excellent claim on the title of best quarterback ever. He has the highest quarterback rating, the highest passing percentage, and the lowest interception percentage in NFL history. He holds NFL records for most seasons with over 3,000 passing yards (6) and most consecutive 300-yard passing games in a season (5, set in 1982). For five seasons, from 1980 to 1984, he completed more than 50 percent of his passes in every single game. He has also been named to the Pro Bowl seven times.

Even more important than his individual records, Montana is a winner. From 1980 through 1990, the 49ers won four Super Bowls and eight NFC West titles. During these years, the team had nine winning seasons and won 70 percent of its games.

Montana has been particularly spectacular in Super Bowl play. He has been named Super Bowl MVP three times. He has thrown 11 Super Bowl touchdowns and passed for 1,142 yards, a Super Bowl record. He also has the most Super Bowl pass completions (77) and the highest completion percentage (68) of all time. Most remarkably, he has made 122 pass attempts in the Super Bowl. None have been intercepted.

Joe Montana's greatness on the football field comes from a mixture of toughness, finesse, quickness, and unbelievable passing accuracy. Plus, he is a brilliant clutch player. So far in his NFL career, Montana has led his team to an extraordinary total of 29 fourth-quarter come-from-behind victories.

George Siefert believes that Joe Montana is "the greatest quarterback of all time." Countless players and coaches have expressed similar sentiments. *USA Today* readers selected Joe as the sports star they would most like to be. But perhaps it is the inhabitants of the small Montana town of Ismay (population 22) who have paid Montana the highest compliment. They recently voted to rename their town "Joe."

JOE MONTANA:
A CHRONOLOGY

1956   Born in New Eagle, Pennsylvania

1974   Accepts scholarship to play football at the University of Notre Dame

1975   Earns nickname as "The Comeback Kid" after leading two thrilling come-from-behind victories as a backup quarterback

1977   Leads Notre Dame to a Cotton Bowl victory and the number one national college football ranking

1979   Drafted in the third round by the San Francisco 49ers

1981   Named the 49ers' starting quarterback before beginning of the season; throws "The Catch" to Dwight Clark; wins Super Bowl MVP award

1984   Leads 49ers to a 15-1 record; wins second Super Bowl MVP trophy

1986   Overcomes potentially career-ending back surgery and returns to play football for the 49ers

1988   Reestablishes himself as 49ers starting quarterback; leads 49ers to a dramatic comeback victory in Super Bowl XXIII with a last-minute touchdown drive

1989   Compiles highest single-season quarterback rating ever; named MVP of the NFL by the Associated Press; wins third Super Bowl MVP award

1990   Named MVP by the Associated Press for the second straight year

1991   Injures elbow; misses all but one game in 1991 and 1992 seasons

1993   Traded to Kansas City Chicfs; leads them to their best postseason showing since 1970

STATISTICS

JOE MONTANA

YEAR	TEAM	G	ATT	CMP	YDS	PCT	INT	TD
1979	SF	1	23	13	96	.565	0	1
1980	SF	7	273	176	1795	**.645**	9	15
1981	SF	16	488	311	3565	**.637**	12	19
1982	SF	9	**346**	213	2613	.616	11	**17**
1983	SF	16	515	332	3910	.645	12	26
1984	SF	15	432	279	3630	.646	10	28
1985	SF	15	494	303	3653	**.613**	13	27
1986	SF	8	307	191	2236	.622	9	8
1987	SF	11	398	266	3054	**.668**	13	**31**
1988	SF	13	397	238	2981	.599	10	18
1989	SF	13	386	271	3521	**.702**	8	26
1990	SF	15	520	321	3944	.617	16	26
1991	SF	—INJURED—						
1992	SF	1	21	15	126	.714	0	2
1993	KC	11	298	181	2144	.607	7	13
TOTALS		151	4898	3095	27368	**.632**	130	257

G   games
ATT   attempts
CMP   completions
YDS   yards
PCT   percent
INT   interceptions
TD   touchdowns

**Bold indicates
league-leading statistics**

records set:
most completed consecutive passes: 22
highest passing percentage, career: .632
lowest interception percentage, career: .027
most seasons with over 3,000 yards passing: 6
most games with 300+ yards passing, consecutive: 5
most touchdown passes: Super Bowl, game: 5
most consecutive completed passes, Super Bowl: 13
most passing yards, Super Bowl, game: 357
most pass attempts without an interception, Super Bowl, game: 35
most pass attempts without an interception, Super Bowl, career:122
most passing yards, Super Bowl, career: 1142
most touchdown passes, Super Bowl, career: 11
highest completion rate, Super Bowl, career: .680
most times named Super Bowl MVP: 3

SUGGESTIONS FOR FURTHER READING

Appleman, Marc. *Joe Montana.* Boston: Little, Brown and Company, 1991.

Arneson, D.J. *Football's Awesome Quarterbacks.* Racine, WI: Western Publishing Company, 1991.

Brenner, Richard J. *Joe Montana, Jerry Rice.* Syosset, NY: East End Publishing, 1990.

Gutmen, Bill. *Great Moments in Pro Football.* New York: Pocket Books, 1986.

Holmstrom, John. *Dan Marino, Joe Montana.* New York: Avon Books, 1985.

Italia, Bob. *Joe Montana.* Edina, MN: Abdo and Daughters, 1992.

Kavanagh, Jack. *Joe Montana.* Hillside, NJ: Enslow Publishers, 1992.

Montana, Joe, and Bob Raissman. *Audibles: My Life in Football.* New York: Avon Books, 1986.

Raber, Thomas R. *Joe Montana: Comeback Quarterback.* Minneapolis, MN: Lerner Publications, 1989.

Schoor, Gene. *100 Years of Notre Dame Football.* New York: William Morrow and Co., 1987.

Tuckman, Michael W., and Jeff Schultz. *The San Francisco 49ers: Team of the Decade.* Rocklin, CA: Prima Publishing & Communications, 1990.

ABOUT THE AUTHOR

Paul Wiener is a freelance writer and a passionate sports fan. In his spare time, he is also a lawyer. A graduate of Columbia University and Harvard Law School, he and his wife Elizabeth live in New York City.

INDEX

PICTURE CREDITS
AP/Wide World Photos: pp. 2, 8, 42, 54; UPI/Bettmann Newsphotos: 13, 25, 26, 28, 30, 32, 36, 41, 45, 48, 51; courtesy Paul Zolack, Ringgold High School: 14, 18; Courtesy University of Notre Dame: 20; Bill Fox Sports Photos, courtesy San Francisco 49ers: 52; Reuters/Bettmann: 58.